12-15 / $28.95

Thinking Critically: Distracted Driving

Carla Mooney

San Diego, CA

About the Author

Carla Mooney is the author of many books for young adults and children. She lives in Pittsburgh, Pennsylvania, with her husband and three children.

For more information, contact:
ReferencePoint Press, Inc.
PO Box 27779
San Diego, CA 92198
www. ReferencePointPress.com

Picture Credits:
Maury Aaseng, 9; Steve Zmina, 17, 22, 30, 35, 41, 46, 55, 61

LIBRARY OF CONGRESS CATALOGING-IN-PUBLICATION DATA

Mooney, Carla, 1970-
  Thinking critically. Distracted driving / by Carla Mooney.
      pages cm. -- (Thinking critically)
  Includes bibliographical references and index.
  ISBN-13: 978-1-60152-780-6 (hardback : alk. paper)
  ISBN-10: 1-60152-780-2 (hardback : alk. paper)
  1. Traffic safety--United States--Juvenile literature. 2. Automobile drivers--United States--Psychology--Juvenile literature 3. Distraction (Psychology)--Juvenile literature I. Title. II. Title: Distracted driving.
  HE5614.2.M54 2015
  363.12'51--dc23
                                                                          2014035194

Contents

Foreword

"Literacy is the most basic currency of the knowledge economy we're living in today." Barack Obama (at the time a senator from Illinois) spoke these words during a 2005 speech before the American Library Association. One question raised by this statement is: What does it mean to be a literate person in the twenty-first century?

E.D. Hirsch Jr., author of *Cultural Literacy: What Every American Needs to Know*, answers the question this way: "To be culturally literate is to possess the basic information needed to thrive in the modern world. The breadth of the information is great, extending over the major domains of human activity from sports to science."

But literacy in the twenty-first century goes beyond the accumulation of knowledge gained through study and experience and expanded over time. Now more than ever literacy requires the ability to sift through and evaluate vast amounts of information and, as the authors of the Common Core State Standards state, to "demonstrate the cogent reasoning and use of evidence that is essential to both private deliberation and responsible citizenship in a democratic republic."

The Thinking Critically series challenges students to become discerning readers, to think independently, and to engage and develop their skills as critical thinkers. Through a narrative-driven, pro/con format, the series introduces students to the complex issues that dominate public discourse—topics such as gun control and violence, social networking, and medical marijuana. All chapters revolve around a single, pointed question such as Can Stronger Gun Control Measures Prevent Mass Shootings?, or Does Social Networking Benefit Society?, or Should Medical Marijuana Be Legalized? This inquiry-based approach introduces student researchers to core issues and concerns on a given topic. Each chapter includes one part that argues the affirmative and one part that argues the negative—all written by a single author. With the single-author format the predominant arguments for and against an issue can be synthesized into clear, accessible discussions supported by details and evidence including relevant facts, direct quotes, current examples, and statistical illustrations. All volumes include focus questions to guide students as they read each pro/con discussion, a list of key facts, and an annotated list of related organizations and websites for conducting further research.

The authors of the Common Core State Standards have set out the particular qualities that a literate person in the twenty-first century must have. These include the ability to think independently, establish a base of knowledge across a wide range of subjects, engage in open-minded but discerning reading and listening, know how to use and evaluate evidence, and appreciate and understand diverse perspectives. The new Thinking Critically series supports these goals by providing a solid introduction to the study of pro/con issues.

High-Tech Distractions

In San Francisco, Shane Walker slides into the driver's seat of his Toyota Prius. He puts on his Google Glass, a pair of lightweight glasses that have a tiny computer built into the lens. The computer keeps him connected to e-mail, phone calls, texts, and other notifications. Walker turns on the Global Positioning System (GPS) app in his Google Glass and starts to drive. The Glass's computer shows his route as a thin blue line and a triangle in the upper right corner of the lens. "Google did a good job of making it nonintrusive, so it's not directly in your line of sight," says Walker. As he drives the streets of San Francisco, Glass streams historical facts about the area around him. Walker insists the text does not distract him while driving. "The layer is transparent, so your eye does a good job of seeing through it while also staring at it,"[1] he says.

Introduced to the general public in 2014, Google Glass is a type of wearable technology that displays information like a hands-free smartphone. Wearers communicate with Glass through touch or voice commands. Glass also has a camera that can take pictures or record video of what wearers are seeing. Wearers can tap the side of Glass to start recording or wink to take a picture. With another tap, they can share the video or pictures with friends. Stroking the Glass frame with a finger enables wearers to flip through stored photos.

While Google Glass is attracting public attention—it was named one of *Time* magazine's best inventions in 2012—many people are concerned about the risk Glass and other high-tech devices pose on the road. Eight states, including Delaware, are considering legislation to ban Glass while driving. Delaware state representative Joseph Miro says that he introduced legislation to ban Glass while driving in his state because of the risk it presents. "I'm not against Google or Google Glass. It may have a place in society," says Miro. "My issue is that while you are driving, you should have nothing that is going to impede the concentration of the driver."[2]

Google disagrees with efforts to prohibit drivers from using their device; company representatives say that Glass can improve driver safety—especially when the alternative is drivers peering down at their phones while at the wheel. "It's actually not distracting, and it allows you—rather than looking down at your phone, you're looking up and you're engaging with the world around you," says Google representative Chris Dale. "It was specifically designed to do that: to get you the technology you need, just when you need it, but then to get out of your way."[3] The company advises drivers to follow state laws when using the device in the car.

Some scientists caution that although drivers may believe that they are being careful, they are underestimating the effect multitasking has on their ability to drive. Earl Miller, a professor of neuroscience at Massachusetts Institute of Technology, says that when a driver multitasks with a device like Glass, his or her brain fills in the gaps in view with memories of what was seen a half second earlier. "You think you're monitoring the road at the same time, when actually what you're doing [is] you're relying on your brain's prediction that nothing was there before, half a second ago—that nothing is there now," he says. "But that's an illusion. It can often lead to disastrous results."[4]

What Is Distracted Driving?

The widespread use of electronic devices by drivers, especially cell phones, has increased concerns about distracted driving. In April 2013 the US Department of Transportation (DOT) released distracted driving guidelines that included recommendations on how and when a driver should use certain built-in electronic devices. For example, DOT recommends that manual text entry should be locked out and inaccessible to drivers while they are driving. According to the National Highway Traffic Safety Administration (NHTSA), additional guidelines covering the use of portable devices and speech-control devices will be issued in the future.

Although electronic devices are one of the biggest concerns, distracted driving does not involve only electronic devices. Distracted driving is driving while engaging in any activity that takes the driver's attention away from the road. A driver can be distracted by talking or texting on a cell phone. Drivers can also be distracted by talking to a passenger, applying makeup, eating behind the wheel, or listening to music. In-vehicle technologies such as navigation systems can also distract drivers.

Driver distractions can be classified into three main categories. Visual distractions such as looking at a GPS screen take a driver's eyes off the road. Manual distractions like reaching for a sandwich take a driver's hands off the steering wheel. Cognitive distraction occurs when a driver is not mentally focused on the task of driving. Drivers can be cognitively distracted while talking on a hands-free cell phone. Texting while driving is one of the most dangerous distractions because it combines visual, manual, and cognitive distractions.

A Nationwide Problem

Distracted driving is a nationwide problem. At any given moment in the United States, approximately 660,000 drivers are using cell phones or other electronic devices behind the wheel, according to the NHTSA. A distracted driver reading or sending a text message might miss seeing a pedestrian or red light. Drivers who are focused more on their phone conversations than on the road sometimes miss exits or turns and try to make risky last-minute corrections. Some weave in and out of driving lanes as they reach for food or apply makeup.

All of these driver distractions make motor vehicle accidents more likely to happen. In some cases distractions result in serious injury and death. According to the Centers for Disease Control and Prevention, nationwide more than 9 people are killed every day and 1,060 more injured in vehicle crashes that involve a distracted driver. The frequency and duration of a distraction can also affect crash risk. Even if a task is less distracting, like changing a radio station, if a driver repeatedly fiddles with the radio or focuses on it for several seconds, the distraction becomes more dangerous.

States Against Texting and Driving

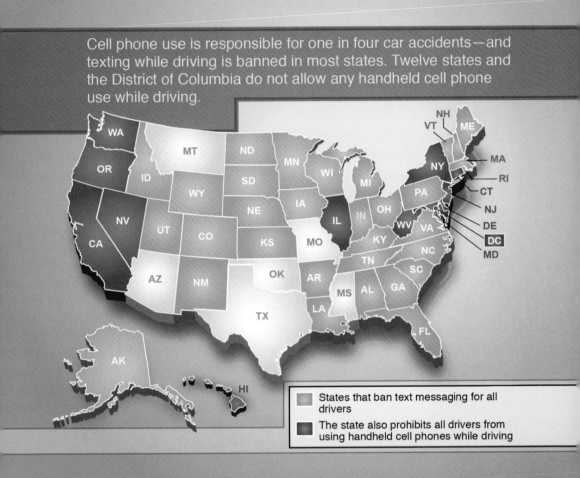

Cell phone use is responsible for one in four car accidents—and texting while driving is banned in most states. Twelve states and the District of Columbia do not allow any handheld cell phone use while driving.

States that ban text messaging for all drivers

The state also prohibits all drivers from using handheld cell phones while driving

Source: Governors Highway Safety Association, "Distracted Driving Laws," October 2014. www.ghsa.org.

Risk Factors

Some distractions are riskier than others and are more likely to lead to an accident. Texting is one of the riskiest distractions behind the wheel. According to the Virginia Tech Transportation Institute (VTTI), drivers who text are twenty-three times more likely to crash than nontexting drivers. Dialing a handheld cell phone also carries a high level of risk. According to VTTI, drivers who dialed phones were 2.8 times more likely to crash than nondistracted drivers. And while talking on the phone, some conversations can be riskier than others. According to researchers at East Tennessee State University, drivers involved in an emotional call engaged in significantly more dangerous driving behaviors than drivers on a mundane call. Driver age and experience can also contribute to the risk of distracted driving. Drivers under age twenty are generally less experienced than older drivers at operating a vehicle and safely dealing with unexpected hazards. Younger drivers are also more likely to engage in distracting behavior such as talking on a cell phone or texting. A study published in January 2014 in the *New England Journal of Medicine* studied the effect distractions had on newly licensed drivers aged sixteen and seventeen. Researchers found that eating almost tripled the risk for a crash, and texting or looking at an object on the side of the road quadrupled crash risk. Dialing a cell phone was the most dangerous activity, increasing the risk of a crash eightfold. "When young people engage in tasks that take their eyes away from the roadway, they're increasing their risk dramatically," says the study's lead author, Charlie Klauer, a research scientist at Virginia Polytechnic Institute and State University. "Kids need to have their eyes forward. To add any other distraction into this is really increasing the risk."[5]

Current Legislation

In response to concerns about distracted driving, many states have enacted laws to regulate the use of electronic devices, especially cell phones. As of August 2014, forty-four states and the District of Columbia had banned text messaging for all drivers. An additional four states had banned text messaging by novice drivers. In addition to the texting bans, fourteen states and the District of Columbia prohibit all drivers from using handheld cell phones for any reason while driving, and thirty-eight states prohibit novice drivers from using all cell phones—whether handheld or hands free. In addition, some cities and counties have passed their own distracted driving laws.

The goal of all of these laws is to improve highway safety and reduce the number of crashes caused by distracted driving. How well they work is not yet clear, however. According to the Association for the Advancement of Automotive Medicine, an organization focused on limiting injuries from motor vehicle crashes, states that have banned handheld cell phone use by drivers have seen many drivers switch to hands-free phones or stop using them altogether. On the other hand, bans on all phone use by novice drivers do not seem to have had an effect on crashes involving young drivers. A 2010 study by the Highway Loss Data Institute concluded that texting bans did not reduce collision claims filed with auto insurance companies. With such conflicting data, many people believe that further research is needed to better understand the effect of legislation on distracted driving behavior.

Every day more distractions compete for drivers' attention. Sometimes these distractions can have serious consequences that lead to injury or death. "Distracted driving is an epidemic. While we've made progress in the past three years by raising awareness about this risky behavior, the simple fact is people are continuing to be killed and injured—and we can put an end to it,"[6] says US Secretary of Transportation Ray LaHood. Most people agree that keeping the roads safe for everyone is a worthy goal. How to achieve this goal in an age of on-the-go technology, however, is up for debate.

Chapter One

Do Hands-Free Devices Enhance Driver Safety?

Hands-Free Devices Enhance Driver Safety

- Hands-free devices make it possible for drivers to drive and talk without taking their eyes off the road or their hands off the steering wheel.
- Integrated voice-based systems eliminate the need to manually manipulate cell phones.
- The general public and state legislators support the use of hands-free devices to improve road safety.
- Visual and manual distractions caused by operating a handheld device are responsible for more accidents than any mental distraction that may be caused by a hands-free device.

The Debate at a Glance

Hands-Free Devices Do Not Enhance Driver Safety

- Hands-free devices give drivers a false sense of security.
- The real distraction is talking on the telephone while driving; the device is a side issue.
- There is little evidence that hands-free devices reduce accident rates and improve road safety.
- In some cases hands-free devices have been found to increase driver distraction.

Hands-Free Devices Enhance Driver Safety

"Ford believes hands-free, voice-activated technology significantly reduces that risk by allowing drivers to keep their hands on the wheel and eyes on the road."

—Pete Lawson, vice president of government affairs, Ford Motor Company.

Quoted in *USA Today*, "Ford Backs Ban on Hand-Held Phones While Driving," July 11, 2011. http://content.usatoday.com.

Consider these questions as you read:

1. Taking into account the facts and ideas presented in this discussion, how persuasive is the argument that hands-free devices enhance driver safety? Which arguments are strongest, and why?
2. Do you think that there is ever a reason to use a cell phone behind the wheel? Why or why not?
3. Do you think this argument will change how you use hands-free devices? Why or why not?

Editor's note: The discussion that follows presents common arguments made in support of this perspective, reinforced by facts, quotes, and examples taken from various sources.

Driving is a visual activity. Any distractions that pull a driver's eyes away from the road increase the risk of a crash. When drivers look at something other than the road—to punch in a phone number or type or read a text, for example—they are more likely to miss slowing traffic, red lights and stop signs, pedestrians, and unexpected road hazards. Drivers who fail to watch the road are likely to have difficulty responding quickly and safely to unexpected situations.

Driving also requires the use of one's hands for steering—and in some cases for shifting gears. Traffic safety officials say drivers should hold the wheel with one hand at the nine o'clock position and the other hand at the three o'clock position. Holding a cell phone with one hand and the steering wheel with the other is a safety hazard. If a child ran out into the road unexpectedly, for instance, a driver would have a harder time turning the steering wheel quickly and maintaining control of the car with only one hand on the wheel. And drivers who control the steering wheel with their knees to free up their hands for texting pose an even greater risk on the road.

Hands-free mobile devices offer a safe alternative for drivers who wish to talk and drive. Such devices eliminate the need for holding a phone or looking at it to punch in a number. Instead, drivers use a Bluetooth, headset, or speakerphone to make and receive phone calls. Voice controls allow drivers to dial a number without using their hands. "The most effective action drivers can take to reduce risks is to place their mobiles in approved cradles affixed to the dashboard or windscreen so they are looking at the road ahead and not glancing down when making a call," says Chris Althaus, chief executive officer (CEO) of the Australian Mobile Telecommunications Association. "Our advice to drivers is based on the latest real world driving research that shows taking your eyes off the road to reach for a phone, dial or read and write text messages significantly increases the risks of crashing." Althaus adds, "We also recommend drivers use a Bluetooth hands-free device or speakerphone when driving and to use smartphone features like single-button dialing or voice-activated calling so they can keep their eyes on the road ahead."[7]

> "Our advice to drivers is based on the latest real world driving research that shows taking your eyes off the road to reach for a phone, dial or read and write text messages significantly increases the risks of crashing."[7]
>
> —Chris Althaus, CEO of the Australian Mobile Telecommunications Association.

Handheld Devices Increase Crash Risk

Multiple studies have shown that manually operating a cell phone while driving distracts drivers and can increase the risk of crashing. In a 2013

VTTI study, researchers found that tasks such as reaching for a phone, dialing, and texting greatly increased a driver's risk of crash. Researchers put GPS systems, radar, cameras, and other equipment into the cars of novice and experienced drivers, who then drove the cars for twelve to eighteen months. The study found that text messaging, browsing, and dialing cell phones caused drivers to look away from the road for the longest periods of time. Tasks needed to complete a phone call, such as reaching for the phone, looking up a contact, and dialing the number, tripled the crash risk.

Text messaging with a handheld cell phone is one of the most dangerous distractions in the car. According to VTTI researchers, a driver who is texting is twenty-three times more likely to have a crash or a near-crash than a driver who is not texting. The danger of texting is so high because texting drivers look away from the road for an average of 4.6 seconds. That may not seem like a long time. Another way to think of this gap is to envision traveling the length of a football field at 55 miles per hour (88.5 kph) with closed eyes. That is the distance a car driving at that speed goes in 4.6 seconds—and a lot can go wrong in that short span of time.

Integrated Voice-Based Systems

While earlier hands-free systems allowed drivers to simply talk on their phones without using their hands, new integrated voice-based systems enable drivers to receive and send text messages hands free. These systems operate with voice commands, eliminating the need for drivers to manipulate cell phones. Drivers can place phone calls, use GPS, and send text messages entirely hands free, improving driver safety.

Automaker Ford has embraced integrated voice systems as a way to reduce dangerous texting while driving. Beginning in 2012, Ford installed its voice-based SYNC technology, an integrated voice-operated communications and entertainment system, in many Ford models. The SYNC voice-activated system connects to a driver's cell phone via Bluetooth technology. When a text is received, SYNC sends an alert, reads it aloud, and allows the driver to choose a prewritten response, all without his or her hands leaving the steering wheel. Ford says that its voice-control technology was developed by research that showed that "hands-free, voice-based interfaces offer advantages over handheld or visual-manual interfaces for command or data entry while driving and reduce the risk of visual driver distractions."[8] For example, during testing, drivers who used SYNC to select a song on their radio took their eyes off the road for a significantly shorter amount of time than drivers who used manually operated radios.

Public Support of Hands-Free Devices

The American public has embraced hands-free technology as a safer way to use cell phones in the car. According to a 2014 poll by the National Safety Council, 80 percent of drivers said they believe using a hands-free device is safer than using a handheld phone. In addition, 70 percent of drivers said that they had made the switch to hands-free devices for safety reasons. Lynford Morton of Bowie, Maryland, is one driver who uses a hands-free phone because he believes it is safer. "Yeah, I think it does make a difference,"[9] Morton says.

Looking to reduce accidents and improve safety, legislators in fourteen states and the District of Columbia, as of August 2014, had banned the use of handheld phones while driving and encouraged the use of hands-free devices. Legislators in several other states are also considering banning handheld devices. In 2014 Wisconsin legislators introduced a bill that requires a hands-free device when using a cell phone while driving. One of the bill's sponsors, State Representative Peter Barca, says he believes it will save lives. "There have been a large number of studies that have been conducted—the State Patrol, insurance companies, Triple A," says Barca. "All the experts in this field have indicated that this is the type of legislation that clearly makes an enormous difference in terms of reducing the number of crashes and saving lives."[10]

Role of Mental Distractions in Accidents Exaggerated

Although those who oppose the use of hands-free technology claim that the mental distraction caused by these devices puts everyone on the road

Hands-Free Devices Reduce Injuries and Fatalities

Hands-free phones are safer than handheld phones on the road. Statistics in California bear this out. According to a 2012 report by the Safe Transportation Research and Education Center (SafeTREC) at the University of California at Berkeley, road safety in California has dramatically improved since July 2008, when a ban on handheld cell phone use by drivers went into effect. An analysis of accidents in the state for the two years before and after the ban showed that injuries and fatalities linked to handheld cell phone use fell by almost 50 percent after the ban was enacted.

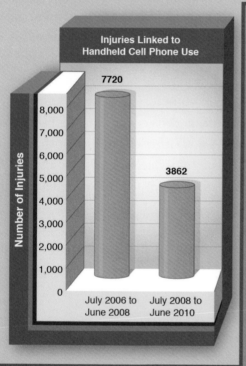

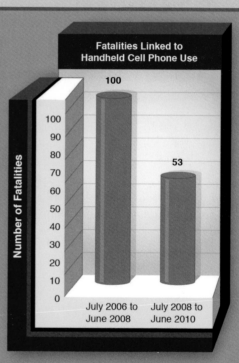

Source: David Ragland, "Descriptive Analyses of Traffic Fatalities and Injuries Before and After California's Law Banning Handheld Cell Phone Use While Driving Was Implemented July 1, 2008," Safe Transportation Research and Education Center, March 2, 2012. http://safetrec.berkeley.edu.

at risk, the visual and manual distraction of handheld devices actually has a much greater role in motor vehicle accidents.

According to a one-hundred-car study conducted by VTTI, visual distractions that cause drivers to look away from the road for more than a few seconds are a factor in 80 percent of distracted driving accidents. "Many distractions increase the relative risk of crashes and near-crashes, and distractions that require drivers to take their eyes off the road are potentially more of a safety problem than purely cognitive distractions,"[11] says the NHTSA.

In today's world people have become reliant on cell phones and portable electronic technology, keeping these devices with them at work, at home, and in the car. When used in cars, handheld devices significantly distract drivers and have become a safety hazard, leading to accident, injury, and death in some cases. Despite knowing these risks, drivers continue to use cell phones and other electronics in the car. Hands-free devices offer a safer alternative, minimizing driver distraction and allowing drivers to keep their eyes and hands where they belong.

> "Many distractions increase the relative risk of crashes and near-crashes, and distractions that require drivers to take their eyes off the road are potentially more of a safety problem than purely cognitive distractions."[11]
>
> —National Highway Traffic Safety Administration.

Hands-Free Devices Do Not Enhance Driver Safety

"Hands-free is not a safety 'silver bullet' and . . . talking on a cell phone while driving is dangerous, no matter whether hand-held or hands-free."

—Lon Anderson, AAA Mid-Atlantic's managing director of public and government affairs.

Quoted in NBC Washington, "AAA: Hands-Free Devices Distract Drivers," June 12, 2013. www.nbc washington.com.

Consider these questions as you read:

1. Taking into account the facts and ideas presented in this discussion, how persuasive is the argument that hands-free devices do not enhance driver safety? Which arguments are strongest, and why?
2. Do you think being mentally distracted is a significant factor in distracted driving crashes? Explain your answer.
3. Why do you think speech-to-text systems have been found to be extremely distracting while driving? Explain your answer.

Editor's note: The discussion that follows presents common arguments made in support of this perspective, reinforced by facts, quotes, and examples taken from various sources.

Driver distraction is a serious and sometimes deadly problem on the road. When a driver's concentration shifts away from the road, even for a split second, the distraction can lead to accident, injury, and death. According to the NHTSA, more than 3,300 people were killed in distraction-related crashes in 2012. That same year an estimated 421,000 additional people were injured in motor vehicle crashes involving a distracted driver, a 9 percent increase over 2011.

Using cell phones or other portable electronic devices while driving is a significant factor in distracted driving accidents. According to a 2014

National Safety Council report, the use of cell phones caused 26 percent of all car accidents in the United States. Hands-free devices such as ear-pieces, dashboard systems, and speakerphones do little to reduce driver distractions. Instead of putting on a hands-free earpiece, drivers should simply put down their phones.

False Sense of Security

Hands-free devices lull drivers into believing that they can use cell phones and other electronic devices safely while driving. A 2014 poll by the National Safety Council found that eight out of ten drivers in the United States believe that hands-free devices are safer than handheld devices in the car. In addition, 70 percent of the poll participants said that they chose to use hands-free devices because of safety concerns. Unfortunately, these views are misguided. David Teater, senior director of Transportation Strategic Initiatives at the National Safety Council, explains:

> While many drivers honestly believe they are making the safe choice by using a hands-free device, it's just not true. The problem is the brain does not truly multi-task. Just like you can't read a book and talk on the phone, you can't safely operate a vehicle and talk on the phone. With some state laws focusing on hand-held bans and carmakers putting hands-free technology in vehicles, no wonder people are confused.[12]

Talking on a telephone, whether using a handheld device or a hands-free system, requires a driver's attention. Divided attention means drivers are slower to react to changing road conditions and unexpected hazards. Even with hands-free systems, drivers still have an increased risk of being in an accident.

Distracting the Brain

The reason for this has to do with how the brain works. Research shows that when performing multiple tasks such as driving and talking on the phone, the brain decreases its performance of each task. This occurs because talking on the phone uses some of the same brain areas as driving; these are the areas that control attention, planning, and language. Because the brain cannot perform both tasks at the same time, it quickly switches back and forth between the two tasks, performing neither at 100 percent. According to the National Safety Council, the brain areas that process moving visual images experience decreased activity by up to one-third when a driver listens or talks on a cell phone. As a result, the driver's field of vision narrows, which can lead to drivers missing up to 50 percent of the images around them.

A 2013 AAA Foundation for Traffic Safety study explored the effect hands-free devices have on a driver's mental workload. Cognitive distraction expert and University of Utah psychology professor David Strayer and a team of researchers measured brain waves, eye movement, and other metrics to assess what happens to a driver's mental workload when attempting to do multiple activities while driving. The researchers found that when mental workload and distractions increased, driver reaction time slowed and brain function was compromised. Drivers also scanned the road less frequently and were more likely to miss visual cues. "Don't assume that if your eyes are on the road and your hands are on the wheel that you are unimpaired. If you don't pay attention then you are a potential hazard on the roadway,"[13] says Strayer, the study's lead author.

The researchers said the more complicated the task, the more distracting it was, and the more likely it was to cause an accident. "These findings reinforce previous research that hands-free is not risk-free," says AAA Foundation for Traffic Safety president and CEO Peter Kissinger. "Increased mental workload and cognitive distractions can lead to a type of tunnel vision or inattention blindness where motorists don't see potential hazards right in front of them."[14]

Hands-free texting also distracts the brain, impairing driver performance. A 2013 study funded by the DOT found that hands-free texting

> "While many drivers honestly believe they are making the safe choice by using a hands-free device, it's just not true."[12]
>
> —David Teater, senior director of Transportation Strategic Initiatives at the National Safety Council.

Drivers' Abilities Decrease Even with Hands-Free Devices

Hands-free devices for making phone calls or sending texts are not safer for drivers than handheld devices. A 2013 study sponsored by the AAA Foundation for Traffic Safety reported that drivers' abilities decreased as distraction in the car increased, even when using hands-free devices. Researchers reported that drivers (using driving simulators) experienced an increased brake reaction time, even when using a hands-free phone.

Average Brake Reaction Time

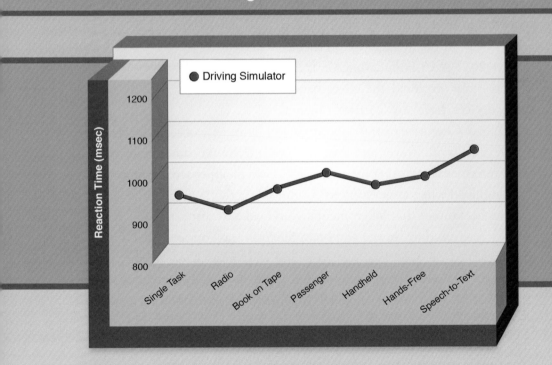

Source: AAA Foundation for Traffic Safety, "Measuring Cognitive Distraction in the Automobile," June 2013. www.aaafoundation.org.

distracted drivers just as much as texting with a handheld device. In the study, participants drove on a closed course while typing text messages manually or sending them using hands-free voice-activated systems. Both methods doubled driver reaction times. Worse still, it took drivers longer to compose text messages by voice command—meaning the distraction time was longer than if they had just typed the message into their phones.

Hands-Free Devices Add to Distractions

Some hands-free systems may actually increase driver distraction. Automakers have been trying to attract buyers, especially young people, with high-tech dashboard infotainment systems that operate with voice commands to turn on windshield wipers, post Facebook messages, or even order pizza. The automakers claim that voice-command systems are safer because drivers do not have to reach for a phone or look away to dial a number.

The 2013 study funded by the AAA Foundation for Traffic Safety found that these voice-command systems may actually increase driver distraction, with voice-activated texting posing the greatest risk. "These new, speech-based technologies in the car can overload the driver's attention and impair their ability to drive safely," says Strayer. "An unintended consequence of trying to make driving safer—by moving to speech-to-text, in-vehicle systems—may actually overload the driver and make them less safe." High-tech infotainment systems that connect drivers to the Internet and social media could add more dangers. "Just because you can update Facebook while driving doesn't mean that it is safe to do so,"[15] Strayer adds.

> "An unintended consequence of trying to make driving safer—by moving to speech-to-text, in-vehicle systems—may actually overload the driver and make them less safe."[15]
>
> —David Strayer, a psychology professor at the University of Utah.

Crash Risk Unchanged

Despite all the claims that hands-free devices are safer to use while driving, there is little evidence that these devices actually reduce accidents. If they were safer, one would expect the number of motor vehicle crashes and near-crashes to decrease after the bans went into effect. Yet in several states with handheld bans, this did not occur. David Teater, senior director of Transportation Strategic Initiatives at the National Safety Council, says that at least thirty major studies have found that bans of handheld devices did not reduce the number of accidents. This leads many to believe that using a hands-free device is just as risky as using a handheld phone. "The only thing that changes when using hands-free is that one hand goes back on the steering wheel,"[16] says Teater.

Absent evidence that hands-free devices reduce motor vehicle crashes, in 2011 the National Transportation Safety Board (NTSB) recommended a nationwide ban on all use of cell phones and text messaging devices while driving—even those that are hands-free. NTSB members say the ban is necessary because drivers face serious risks whether using hands-free systems or handheld devices. Although the recommendation is nonbinding, it represents the first time a federal agency has called for a complete ban of cell phone use while driving. Deborah Hersman, the NTSB chair, says it is important to make sure people focus on the act of driving. "It's about cognitive distraction. It's about not being engaged at the task at hand," says Hersman. "Lives are being lost in the blink of an eye. You can't take it back, you can't have a do over, and you can't rewind."[17]

Although hands-free devices enable drivers to keep their hands on the steering wheel, they do not solve the ultimate problem: driver distraction. Drivers using cell phones are distracted whether they are holding the phone in their hand or using hands-free systems. "As we push towards these hands-free systems, we may be solving one problem while creating another,"[18] says Joel Cooper, a University of Utah assistant research professor. Hands-free devices are not going to make the roads safer. The solution, clearly, is to just put them away while driving.

Chapter Two

Should Cell Phone Use by Drivers Be Banned?

Cell Phone Use by Drivers Should Be Banned

- Studies have found that cell phones are one of the most dangerous distractions on the road, significantly increasing the risk of accidents and injury.
- Studies show that cell phones are even more dangerous when drivers use them for texting behind the wheel.
- Partial bans, which are confusing and hard to enforce, should be replaced by bans on all cell phone use by drivers.

The Debate at a Glance

Cell Phone Use by Drivers Should Not Be Banned

- Cell phone bans sound good but mean little since many distractions have nothing to do with cell phones.
- Cell phone bans are another example of the nanny state, which seeks to replace individual decision making with government edicts on personal behavior.
- Some states that have implemented bans have experienced an increase in accident rates.
- Because bans are difficult to enforce, there is little incentive for drivers to change their behavior.

Cell Phone Use by Drivers Should Be Banned

"The most important action that state legislatures can take at this time is to institute a complete ban on all handheld cell phone use, which will save lives and greatly simplify police enforcement."

—Jay Winsten, an associate dean at Harvard School of Public Health.

Jay Winsten, "Stopping Distracted Driving: What Will It Take?," *Huffington Post*, November 1, 2013. www.huffingtonpost.com.

Consider these questions as you read:

- Taking into account the facts and ideas presented in this discussion, how persuasive is the argument that cell phone use by drivers should be banned? Which arguments are strongest, and why?
- Do you think that there is ever a reason to use a cell phone behind the wheel? Why or why not?
- What effect, if any, would a total ban have on driver behavior?

Editor's note: The discussion that follows presents common arguments made in support of this perspective, reinforced by facts, quotes, and examples taken from various sources.

Cell phones are one of the leading causes of driver distraction. When a driver's concentration shifts away from the road to a cell phone, the distraction can lead to accident, injury, and death. According to the National Safety Council's 2014 annual injury and fatality report, 26 percent of car accidents in the United States involved drivers talking on cell phones or texting. This number may be even higher because many drivers are unwilling to admit using their phones. To make the nation's roads safer, cell phone use while driving should be prohibited in every state. "Distracted driving laws can and do save lives,"[19] says Joe Simitian, a California state senator.

Dangerous Distraction

Cell phones are a dangerous distraction on the road. Many people have observed the swerving and erratic movements of a car being driven by someone who is using a cell phone. "While a member of the Pawtucket Police Department, I was nearly struck by a driver who was distracted on a cell phone," says Peter Kilmartin, Rhode Island's attorney general. "Texting and distracted driving is now one of the greatest dangers facing drivers on our roads, and is as dangerous, if not more so, than driving drunk."[20]

> "Distracted driving laws can and do save lives."[19]
>
> —Joe Simitian, a California state senator.

In fact, studies have actually confirmed that a driver talking on a phone or texting represents more of a road hazard than a drunk driver. One benchmark study done in 2006 by researchers at the University of Utah used a driving simulator to test how people drive while intoxicated and how they drive while talking on a cell phone. Each of the forty-one adults who took part in the study operated a driving simulator under four conditions: undistracted, using a handheld cell phone, using a hands-free phone, and after drinking enough vodka to raise their blood-alcohol level to 0.08, the legal definition of driving while intoxicated. "We found that people are as impaired when they drive and talk on a cell phone as they are when they drive intoxicated at the legal blood-alcohol limit," says study coauthor Frank Drews, an assistant professor of psychology. "If legislators really want to address driver distraction, then they should consider outlawing cell phone use while driving."[21]

More recent studies have come to a similar conclusion. In 2013 student researchers at Touro University in Vallejo, California, also concluded that cell phone use impaired drivers and slowed their reaction times. The researchers tested drivers on cell phones with law enforcement sobriety tests, the same tests given to drunk driving suspects. Participants were asked to perform three components of the sobriety test—the horizontal gaze test, walk and turn, and the one-leg stand—while wearing a Bluetooth hands-free device. One group talked on the hands-free device, while a second group did not. Researchers found that more than 25 percent of the hands-free participants failed the sobriety tests. "If more and more studies performed demonstrate impairment with these devices then driving laws may have to be changed,"[22] says Eric Ip, Touro associate professor of pharmacy practice.

For novice drivers, cell phone use while driving is even more dangerous. A 2014 study by VTTI found that the risk of a crash or near-miss for young drivers increased sevenfold when they were dialing or reaching for a cell phone. "Our findings indicate that secondary tasks requiring drivers to look away from the road ahead, such as dialing and texting, are significant risk factors for crashes and near-crashes, particularly among novice drivers,"[23] wrote the study's authors.

Some of the crashes caused by cell phone distraction are deadly. On the morning of June 16, 2011, nineteen-year-old Evan Lieberman of Chappaqua, New York, and two other college students were driving to a summer job when another driver hit their car head-on. Lieberman was killed and the other two students injured. The driver, nineteen-year-old Michael Fiddle, was not charged in the deadly crash. In a civil lawsuit, however, an administrative law judge ruled that Fiddle had violated several traffic laws, including texting while driving. The judge suspended Fiddle's driver's license for one year. Ben and Debbie Lieberman, Evan's parents, are urging lawmakers to ban cell phones while driving. They want states to adopt and enforce stiff penalties for cell phone use while driving. "If we can save one life, it will be worth it,"[24] says Ben Lieberman.

> "If more and more studies performed demonstrate impairment with these devices then driving laws may have to be changed."[22]
>
> —Eric Ip, Touro associate professor of pharmacy practice.

Texting Increases Road Dangers

Texting while driving is perhaps the most serious road hazard, especially where teen drivers are concerned. In 2012 researchers at the University of Washington's Harborview Injury Prevention and Research Center tested the performance of teen drivers who were sending or reading texts while behind the wheel. The researchers found that no matter where the teen participants held their phones—whether in their lap or to the side or at the top of the steering wheel—their driving skills were impaired. The texting teens were about four to six times more likely to drift out of their lanes and were twice as likely to have near misses with cars and pedestrians.

A texting teen from Kansas City, Missouri, caused a deadly traffic crash in 2012. According to court records, sixteen-year-old Rachel Gannon was looking at her phone and texting when she lost control of her vehicle and slammed into a car driven by seventy-two-year-old Loretta Larimer. Larimer, who had pulled off the road in an attempt to avoid Gannon's out-of-control car, was killed. Larimer's ten-year-old granddaughter, who was also in the car, was injured in the accident.

A Total Ban Required

Despite the many studies confirming the danger of mixing cell phones with driving, as of August 2014 all states allowed at least some cell phone use by drivers. Many states have adopted partial bans. Some ban handheld use but allow hands-free devices. Others ban all cell phone use for novice drivers but allow experienced drivers to use phones. Some states ban texting, but allow phone calls. Even a few cities, such as Flagstaff, Arizona, have joined in by passing their own laws. This is utterly confusing, and many drivers simply choose to ignore the laws and continue to use phones behind the wheel.

For safety's sake the best solution would be to ban all cell phone use by all drivers. The NTSB has already called for a nationwide ban on all cell phone use and text messaging devices while driving. Many people object to such a ban; they argue that cell phones are an essential modern convenience. And in many ways they are—but not on the road. NTSB chair Deborah Hersman expresses this view when she says, "Needless lives are lost on our highways, and for what? Convenience? Death isn't convenient. So we can stay more connected? A fatal accident severs that connection."[25]

Illinois Voters Support Cell Phone Ban

Many drivers are finally realizing the dangers of talking on their phones or texting while driving and are fully behind measures that prohibit such behavior. An Illinois law that went into effect in January 2014 bans the use of handheld cell phones by drivers. A poll conducted shortly before the ban was signed in 2013 reveals that Illinois voters overwhelmingly support the statewide ban.

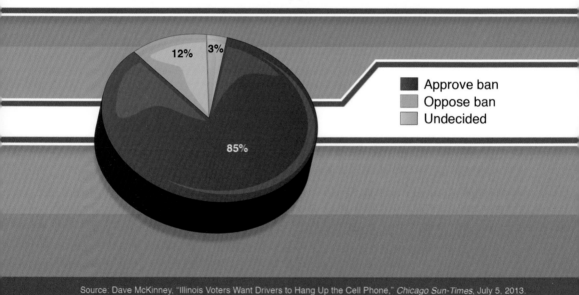

Illinois Voters Support Cell Phone Ban

12%   3%

■ Approve ban
■ Oppose ban
□ Undecided

85%

Source: Dave McKinney, "Illinois Voters Want Drivers to Hang Up the Cell Phone," *Chicago Sun-Times*, July 5, 2013. www.suntimes.com.

Easier Enforcement

A ban on all cell phone use while driving will make enforcement much easier for police. Under current laws, it is difficult for police to determine if a driver is texting, which is banned, or dialing a phone, which may not be banned. Laws that cannot be effectively enforced are useless and will be ignored by drivers. In Pennsylvania, lawmakers banned texting while driving in 2012, but police officers say that the law is difficult to enforce. As a result, few people are cited for violations. "It's difficult to make that arrest due to the current law," says Scranton police chief Carl Graziano. "It's difficult for an officer to discern whether they're texting or looking up numbers on their phone."[26]

The use of cell phones while driving is a dangerous and potentially deadly distraction. Despite the risks, many people continue to talk and text while driving, putting others at risk. A ban on all cell phone use is necessary to keep roads safe for everyone.

Cell Phone Use by Drivers Should Not Be Banned

"Instead of solutions which are voluntary and rely on education and technology, [US transportation secretary Ray] LaHood seeks out the hysterical approach of banning cell phone use outright—this is a solution whose time hasn't come."

—Horace Cooper, a legal commentator and adjunct fellow at the National Center for Public Policy Research.

Quoted in Peter Roff, "Don't Ban Driving with Cell Phones," *U.S. News & World Report*, April 27, 2012. www.usnews.com.

Consider these questions as you read:

1. Taking into account the facts and ideas presented in this discussion, how persuasive is the argument that cell phone use by drivers should not be banned? Which arguments are strongest, and why?
2. Do you think governments are overstepping their bounds by trying to regulate driver behaviors? Why or why not?
3. Are there ways other than banning all cell phone use to reduce distracted driving? Explain your answer.

Editor's note: The discussion that follows presents common arguments made in support of this perspective, reinforced by facts, quotes, and examples taken from various sources.

Laws that ban cell phones while driving are off base; they do not address the real danger, which is driver distraction. Today's drivers face many distractions behind the wheel, with cell phones being only one part of the problem. Drivers are distracted by eating, changing radio stations, talking to passengers, or dealing with children in the backseat. Any of these distractions can lead to accidents, injuries, and death. In fact, a 2013 analysis of fatal crash reports conducted by Erie Insurance found that talking and texting on cell phones was not the leading cause of driver distraction in fatal crashes. "Distracted driving is any activity that takes your eyes off the road, your hands off the wheel, or your mind off your primary task of driving safely," says Doug Smith, an executive at Erie Insurance. "We looked at what law enforcement officers across the country reported when they filled out reports on fatal crashes and the results were disturbing."[27] The analysis found that drivers who were lost in thought or daydreaming were responsible for 62 percent of the fatal distracted driving crashes. Cell phone use was a distant second, responsible for only 12 percent of fatal distracted driving crashes. As this study demonstrates, a ban on cell phone use while driving would not create safer conditions on the road and therefore would be pointless.

In fact, states that prohibit drivers from using cell phones have not seen a reduction in car accidents. As Russ Rader, a spokesperson for the Insurance Institute for Highway Safety in Arlington, Virginia, notes: "Cell phone bans have reduced cell phone use by drivers, but the perplexing thing is that they haven't reduced crashes."[28] Distracted driving has many causes; instead of adopting more laws that address only one small part of the larger problem, states and cities should improve driver education and awareness campaigns.

> "Cell phone bans have reduced cell phone use by drivers, but the perplexing thing is that they haven't reduced crashes."[28]
>
> —Russ Rader, a spokesperson for the Insurance Institute for Highway Safety.

The Nanny State

Those who argue for an all-out ban on talking or texting behind the wheel are misguided. They mistakenly view every instance of cell phone use by drivers as a threat to safety. Clearly this is not the case. For example, a driver who is stopped at a red light can send a quick text to tell a friend that he or she is running late. Similarly, a teen driver who is caught in a huge traffic jam can do the same to allay the fears of a worried parent. These scenarios do not pose a threat to the driver or to other cars on the road. Accidents involving cell phone–using drivers are unfortunate but should not be seen as the norm. As any driver can attest, cell phone use by drivers is rampant. Surely even more accidents would be occurring if this were the heart of the distracted driving problem. Christopher Schrader, a twenty-nine-year-old consultant from San Jose, California, is a longtime cell phone user who considers himself a good driver even when using his phone. "I personally still drive while talking on my cellphone, and I don't feel distracted in any way," he says. "And even crazier, I sometimes even text when I feel it is safe. I've never been in an accident in 13 years of driving and have always used my phone during that time. I personally don't find it difficult to put my focus on the road and have a conversation."[29]

The effort to ban all cell phone use by drivers is one more example of the "nanny state"—a government that makes decisions about personal behavior rather than letting people make those decisions for themselves. Most drivers really are capable of deciding when—and when not—to use a cell phone. Legislation to ban all cell phone use substitutes the state's judgment for the driver's. Current laws do not ban motorists from eating in their cars, even though this is a proven distraction. The same is true for activities such as fiddling with the radio and using dashboard GPS devices, both of which can also distract drivers. The government assumes drivers will use their judgment to decide when and how to engage in such activities. Drivers should have the same rights and responsibilities when it comes to cell phone use.

Bans Increase Crashes

In some cases cell phone bans might actually increase the risk of motor vehicle crashes. According to a Highway Loss Data Institute (HLDI) study, many states that have adopted texting bans have experienced zero reduction in crashes. What the HLDI study found, in fact, is that crashes in these states actually increased. These results were consistent with another HLDI study that found that bans of handheld cell phone use did not decrease crash risk. "Texting bans haven't reduced crashes at all. In a perverse twist, crashes increased in 3 of the 4 states we studied after bans were enacted. It's an indication that texting bans might even increase the risk of

Cell Phone Bans Will Not Fix the Problem

Laws that ban cell phone use by drivers will do little to reduce distracted driving and improve road safety because cell phones are only a small part of the problem. Distracted driving is anything that takes a driver's attention away from the road including eating, talking to passengers, and changing radio stations. According to the National Highway Traffic Safety Administration, only a small number of fatal crashes and fatalities in 2012 actually involved cell phones. The majority of such crashes and fatalities involved other distractions.

Number of Fatal Crashes and Fatalities, 2012

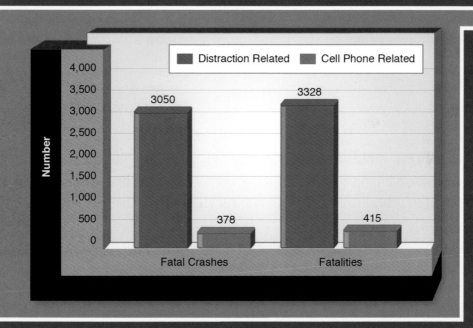

Source: National Highway Traffic Safety Administration, "Distracted Driving 2012," April 2014. www.nrd.nhtsa.dot.gov.

texting for drivers who continue to do so despite the laws,"[30] says Adrian Lund, president of HLDI and the Insurance Institute for Highway Safety.

Lund believes the increase in crashes may have been caused by drivers trying to hide their cell phone use. Using a device that is hidden from view on their lap or vehicle seat causes drivers to look away from the road even longer than when such activities are allowed. Lund explains:

> If drivers were disregarding the bans, then the crash patterns should have remained steady. So clearly drivers did respond to the bans somehow, and what they might have been doing was moving their phones down and out of sight when they texted, in recognition that what they were doing was illegal. This could exacerbate the risk of texting by taking drivers' eyes further from the road and for a longer time.[31]

If texting bans have done little to improve road safety, there is little chance that adding more legislation to ban all cell phone use by drivers will reduce accidents. Instead, more legislation may increase motor vehicle accidents as more people try to hide their phones from law enforcement.

Bans Are Difficult to Enforce

One other problem with efforts to ban cell phone use by drivers is that those charged with enforcing the laws say such laws are mostly unenforceable. In states that prohibit drivers from texting and talking on handheld cell phones, police describe these laws as difficult to enforce. On any given trip, drivers typically glance at the radio or at something on the seat or floor of their car. Police officers say it is hard to know what these drivers are looking at—whether they are using a cell phone or looking at something else. Bans on hands-free devices are not much better. How is an officer to know whether a driver's moving lips are a sign of a prohibited phone conversation, a sing-along with the radio, or even someone just talking to him- or herself? "It would be almost impossible to determine if someone was talking on a phone or exercising their vocal cords," says Captain Donald Melanson of the West Hartford, Connecticut, police department. "That would be much more difficult to enforce, almost to the point where it would be impossible."[32]

Without the ability to enforce bans, legislation has little hope of changing driver behavior. If drivers know that they can use phones without getting caught, there is no incentive for them to stop using phones. Joe Schwieterman, a DePaul University professor who studies people's use of technology while traveling, says that the public would likely ignore laws that ban cell phone use. "It's a little like speeding laws where it will become just culturally acceptable to violate,"[33] he says.

The effort to ban all use of cell phones by drivers addresses only one aspect of a much larger problem. "They're focusing on a single manifestation of distracted driving and banning it," says Lund. "This ignores the endless sources of distraction and relies on banning one source or another to solve the whole problem."[34] Instead of legislation, efforts to educate drivers about the risks of all types of driver distraction are more likely to reduce accidents and improve road safety.

> "They're focusing on a single manifestation of distracted driving and banning it. . . . This ignores the endless sources of distraction and relies on banning one source or another to solve the whole problem."[34]
>
> —Adrian Lund, president of HLDI and the Insurance Institute for Highway Safety.

Chapter Three

Would Stiffer Penalties Reduce Distracted Driving Threats?

Stiffer Penalties Would Reduce Distracted Driving Threats

- Tougher penalties have been effective in changing driver behavior in the past.
- The public supports tougher penalties and enforcement for distracted driving laws.
- States that have implemented stiffer penalties say that these measures are needed to send a message about the serious consequences of distracted driving.

The Debate at a Glance

Stiffer Penalties Would Not Reduce Distracted Driving Threats

- In most jurisdictions existing penalties are sufficient to deter distracted driving and prevent accidents.
- Even with stiffer penalties, distracted driving laws are difficult to enforce and will have little effect on driver behavior.
- The most effective way to change driver behavior and reduce distracted driving is to educate drivers about the risks and consequences of distracted driving.

Stiffer Penalties Would Reduce Distracted Driving Threats

"I think texting while driving is such a dangerous and pervasive problem. . . . I don't think they're going to stop unless there's a severe penalty or until, unfortunately, there's a tragedy."

—Charlene Lima, Rhode Island state representative.

Quoted in Paul J. Spetrini, "RI's Texting While Driving Law Proving Ineffective," GoLocalProv, February 22, 2013. www.golocalprov.com.

Consider these questions as you read:

1. How persuasive is the argument that stiffer penalties would reduce distracted driving threats? Which arguments are strongest, and why?
2. Do you think stiffer penalties will have an effect on driver behavior? Explain your answer.
3. What do you think should be done to address the concerns about distracted driving? Why?

Editor's note: The discussion that follows presents common arguments made in support of this perspective, reinforced by facts, quotes, and examples taken from various sources.

The penalties for distracted driving need to be increased so that drivers are motivated to change their behavior behind the wheel. Often, the penalty for distracted driving is only a small fine. Even when driver distraction causes serious injury or death, drivers face little punishment. In 2011 a driver using a cell phone in Delaware caused an accident that killed a five-year-old boy. The driver walked away with only a $1,000 fine. Significant penalties that include jail time, hefty fines, and loss of a driver's license—similar to the penalties for drunk driving—are desperately needed. Without this, drivers will not give up the distracting behaviors that threaten everyone on the road. New Jersey state senator Dick Codey, a sponsor of a measure to increase fines in his state, says distracted-driving prevention is similar to the drunk-driving campaign of years past. "Our goal is to have people stop injuring each other," he says. "Before, it was a slap on the wrist. What people need is a slap on the face."[35]

Stiffer Penalties Work

Over the years, stiffer penalties have been effective in changing driver behavior. When seat belt laws were first implemented, many drivers were resistant and did not comply. Justin McNaull, director of state relations for AAA, says that when states imposed higher penalties for not buckling up, more motorists obeyed the seat belt laws.

In 2014 researchers at the University of Western Ontario in Canada reported that stricter laws and more severe penalties for extreme speeding and aggressive driving dramatically reduced the number of speeding-related deaths and injuries. The researchers studied the impact of laws that took effect in 2007 in Ontario by analyzing government data before and after that change. Under the stricter laws, drivers who exceeded the speed limit by at least 31 miles per hour (50 kph) or who engaged in racing or other dangerous driving behaviors could have their licenses immediately suspended and their cars impounded for seven days. If convicted, the drivers could also face fines of $2,000 to $10,000, license suspensions for up to two years, and up to six months in jail. Drivers convicted of a second offense faced even more severe penalties. The study looked at driving behavior of both male and female drivers. Study author Evelyn Vingilis, a professor in family medicine, epidemiology, and biostatistics, explains the findings: "What we found was a substantial reduction in the number of convictions for extreme speeding for males, and no change for females

> "Our goal is to have people stop injuring each other. . . . Before, it was a slap on the wrist. What people need is a slap on the face."[35]
>
> —New Jersey state senator Dick Codey.

Public Supports Stiffer Penalties for Texting While Driving

Public education will not stop people from texting while driving. What is needed are stiffer penalties—and a 2014 poll from the National Safety Council confirms that the general public supports such penalties. Three types of penalties—points that could lead to higher insurance costs or loss of license, higher penalties for repeat offenders, and large fines—each won support from at least half of respondents. Additionally, many of those surveyed say that they favor more enforcement of existing texting laws.

Poll: What Penalty Would You Like to See for Texting While Driving?

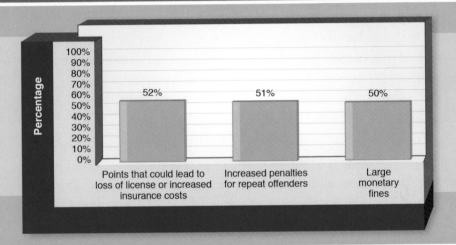

Is Enforcement of Existing Texting Laws Adequate?

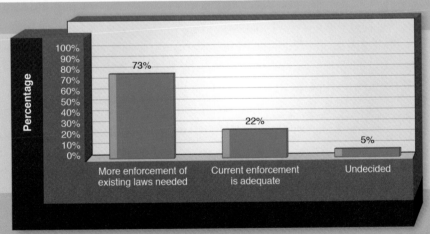

Source: National Safety Council, "Public Ready for Stiffer Penalties for Texting While Driving," June 23, 2014. www.nsc.org.

because they were pretty low anyway. And importantly, we found a significant decrease in the number of motor vehicle casualties of males 16 to 24—quite a significant reduction."[36] Vingilis concluded that the stricter laws and penalties likely discouraged dangerous driving.

The Public Supports Stricter Penalties

Many people are fed up with distracted drivers who refuse to stop talking and texting, at the risk of everyone on the road. "I am so tired of seeing people do it day after day," says Lisa Mendoza, of San Jose, California. Mendoza says that one time when she saw a woman texting while driving, she tried to suggest the woman should put the phone down. "When I motioned that she should stop, she flipped me off,"[37] says Mendoza. Many are concerned that the amount of potential distractions, from smartphones to in-dashboard electronic systems, will only increase in future years.

To get drivers to put down their phones, many people support stricter penalties and enforcement for distracted driving laws. In a 2014 National Safety Council public opinion poll, 73 percent of respondents said they believe there should be more enforcement of existing texting and distracted driving laws. When asked what type of penalties they would like to see for distracted driving, 52 percent of respondents said drivers should receive points on their license, similar to the points received when a driver gets into an accident or gets a traffic citation. After a certain number of points, insurance costs increase, and policies can eventually be canceled. With too many points, a driver can also lose his or her license. About half of respondents (51 percent) said there should be increasingly harsh penalties for repeat offenders. Half also supported large monetary fines. "For years, there has been widespread opposition to texting behind the wheel," says National Safety Council president and CEO Deborah Hersman. "Today, the polls show the public is behind stronger penalties because most people recognize that it will take more than awareness campaigns to stop this dangerous behavior."[38]

States Implement Stiffer Penalties

Some states have already taken steps to implement stiffer penalties for distracted driving. In April 2014 Maryland governor Martin O'Malley signed a bill known as Jake's law, creating stiffer penalties and jail time for drivers who cause a serious or fatal car crash while texting or talking on a cell phone. In 2011 five-year-old Jake Owen was killed when a driver using a cell phone rear-ended Jake's family car. Although the impact killed Jake, the driver walked away with a $1,000 fine. Many people were outraged by the minor fine. "When you take someone's life, when acting recklessly and negligently, there should be more consequences,"[39] says Luke Clippinger, a prosecutor in Anne Arundel County, Maryland, who lives in the Owen family's neighborhood. Under the new law, judges can impose a jail sentence of up to a year in jail and a $5,000 fine. Susan Yum, Jake's mother, says that she hopes tougher penalties will deter people from using their phones and other devices while driving. "It's socially acceptable now," she says

> "For years, there has been widespread opposition to texting behind the wheel. . . . Today, the polls show the public is behind stronger penalties because most people recognize that it will take more than awareness campaigns to stop this dangerous behavior."[38]
>
> —Deborah Hersman, National Safety Council president and CEO.

about distracted driving. "Jake was 5 years old. He shouldn't have died that way. That crash was entirely preventable."[40]

In Nevada, laws that have raised the penalties for fatal accidents involving distracted driving are being put to the test. In March 2014 in Las Vegas, thirty-four-year-old Karen Morris was speeding at 64 miles per hour (103 kph) in a 45-mile-per-hour (72 kph) zone while talking on her cell phone. She ran a red light and crashed into another car. The accident killed two people and seriously injured a third. Morris was charged with three felony counts of reckless driving and two felony counts of involuntary manslaughter. If convicted, she faces up to twenty-six years in jail. Prosecutors say that Morris's distraction was a criminal act. "If you are inattentive because of that cell phone, you are violating due care. . . . And if that contributes to a crash and someone is killed then you have committed a criminal act,"[41] says Nevada prosecutor Gary Booker.

The case is the first of its kind in Nevada and could lead to more distracted drivers who cause serious accidents being charged with a felony. "The underlying facts are that she was speeding, running red lights and talking on a cell phone without paying full time and attention," says Clark County deputy district attorney Mary Brown. "The thing that makes this case memorable is the consequences. It's certainly a first in our area."[42]

Stronger Consequences Send a Message

Tougher penalties and higher fines will grab drivers' attention and make them think seriously about getting rid of distractions. Too many people ignore existing distracted driving and cell phone laws because the penalties for getting caught are minor. "Higher fines send a message that picking up the phone or texting while operating a vehicle is a dangerous distraction, with serious consequences,"[43] says Cynthia Harris, a spokesperson for AAA of Northern California. In order to achieve real change in the public's behavior, tougher penalties for violating distracted driving laws are needed.

Stiffer Penalties Would Not Reduce Distracted Driving Threats

"Distracted driving, in all its forms, can best be addressed through efforts to educate the public on its dangers. Enforcement can be useful to a degree, but banning specific actions is unnecessary."

—National Motorists Organization.

National Motorists Organization, "Distracted Driving Fact Sheet." www.motorists.org.

Consider these questions as you read:

1. How persuasive is the argument that stiffer penalties would not reduce distracted driving threats? Which arguments are strongest, and why?
2. Do you think current penalties for distracted driving are adequate? Why or why not?
3. What do you think should be done to reduce distracted driving? Explain your answer.

Editor's note: The discussion that follows presents common arguments made in support of this perspective, reinforced by facts, quotes, and examples taken from various sources.

Although most people agree that distractions in the car increase the likelihood of accidents and injuries, there is little evidence that stiffer penalties would have a significant effect on driver behavior and reduce distracted driving. Education about the hazards of distracted driving is more likely to motivate drivers to develop good driving habits and improve road safety than harsher punishments. And the need for education is growing. "In the near future, and perhaps for years to come, reducing driver distraction to increase roadway safety is going to be increasingly challenging. As automated functions increase in vehicles, drivers are likely to feel

Enforcement Difficulties Defeat Purpose of Stiffer Penalties

Distracted driving laws are nearly impossible to enforce, rendering stiffer penalties almost meaningless. In states around the country, laws imposing penalties for texting and cell phone use by drivers have fallen short mainly because few people are actually cited for violating the laws. In Kentucky, for instance, a ban on texting for all drivers and cell phone use for drivers under age eighteen took effect in January 2011. Between January 2011 and February 6, 2013, the state only issued 976 citations for texting or using a cell phone while driving. In a state with more than 3.15 million licensed drivers, the risk of a driver getting a citation for texting is about three in ten thousand.

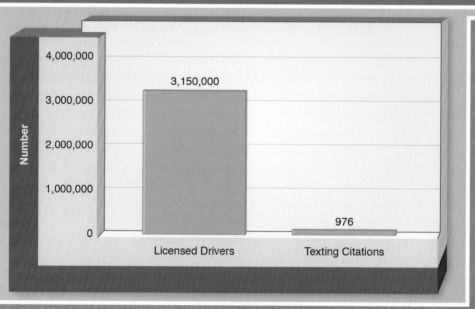

Texting & Cell Phone Citations in Kentucky
January 2011 – February 6, 2013

Source: Beth Musgrave, "Few of Kentucky's 3.15 Million Drivers Cited for Texting While Driving," *Lexington Herald-Leader*, May 5, 2013. www.kentucky.com.

that their attention to the road is less necessary," says C. Raymond Bingham from the University of Michigan Transportation Research Institute in Ann Arbor, Michigan. "Cultural attitudes and values and the public's tolerance for distracted driving need to be targeted by informative and persuasive public health campaigns that make evident the need and create a public demand for individual behavior change."[44]

Current Fines Are Adequate

Laws already exist in many states and even some cities. Drivers who violate these laws face penalties, including fines and license suspensions. In most jurisdictions, existing penalties are sufficient to deter distracted driving. In California, first-time offenders who violate laws that prohibit drivers from texting or using handheld cell phones face a fine of $189. California governor Jerry Brown believes this fine is a powerful deterrent to distracted driving. When the California legislature passed a bill in 2011 to increase penalties for drivers who text or use a handheld cell phone, Brown vetoed the bill. In his veto, Brown wrote, "I certainly support discouraging cellphone use while driving a car, but not ratcheting up the penalties as prescribed by this bill. . . . For people of ordinary means, current fines and penalty assessments should be sufficient deterrent."[45] In 2012 Brown vetoed a second bill that called for higher distracted driving penalties. He said that he doubted increased fines would further improve road safety. "Upping the fines may satisfy the punitive instincts of some, but I severely doubt that it will further reduce violations,"[46] he said.

> "Upping the fines may satisfy the punitive instincts of some, but I severely doubt that it will further reduce violations."[46]
>
> —Jerry Brown, governor of California.

Many California residents agree with Brown. Andrey Abutin from Sunnyvale, California, agrees with the governor's vetoes and says the law should distinguish between safe and unsafe use of cell phones in the car. "Is it any wonder the majority of the public considers this law insulting and absurd, and disregards it accordingly?" says Abutin. "Let's address the real problem here: dangerously distracted drivers, not the people whose only crime is driving while holding a phone in their hand."[47]

Stiffer Penalties Will Not Work Without Enforcement

Even if states toughen penalties for distracted driving, it will have an insignificant effect on driver behavior if police officers cannot enforce the laws. Drivers will have little incentive to change their behavior if the likelihood of being caught is low. For example, New Hampshire passed a ban on text messaging while driving in 2009. The state also has a strict distracted driving law, which imposes fines for eating, applying makeup, and talking on a cell phone while driving. Police officers, however, admit that the laws are hard to enforce. "Would a cop pull somebody over for texting? Probably not, unless the car was swerving all over the road," says Jim Van Dongen, the public information officer for the New Hampshire Department of Safety. "And if the car was swerving all over the road, they would go after it whether the person was texting or driving under the influence. You can't really see from the outside of the car what somebody's doing."[48]

In Rhode Island, where a law against texting while driving was passed in 2009, police officers are finding it difficult to enforce. As a result, the law has had little effect. Between 2009 and February 2013, local and state police officers issued fewer than six hundred tickets to drivers for texting. Rhode Island state representative Charlene Lima admits that the texting law has not been effective. "You see people looking down at stop signs with their phones in their hands, not paying attention to the road, you see people swerving, I think it's still going on," she says. "People don't learn their lesson. They're not getting caught because it's such a difficult thing to catch people doing."[49]

Public Education Changes Driver Behavior

The most effective way to change behavior and stop distracted driving is not to strengthen penalties but to educate each and every driver about the serious risks and consequences of distracted driving. The success of widespread education efforts to inform people about the risks of drunk driving proves that this approach works. In 1988 the Harvard School of Public Health's Center for Health Communication launched the US Designated Driver Campaign. The campaign encouraged people to plan ahead and designate one person who does not drink at all to be the driver for a group of friends. The campaign partnered with television networks and Hollywood studios to spread the message and shift public drinking and driving behavior. The American public embraced the designated driver idea and by 1998, a majority of adults who drink had served as a designated driver or had been driven home by one. "So we know that media campaigns can move the needle on behavior change,"[50] says Jay Winsten, associate dean at the Harvard School of Public Health.

A campaign to warn the public about the dangers of distracted driving can have a similar result. "In order to change people's behaviors, we need to continually educate the public about the dangers of texting while driving,"[51] says Rhode Island attorney general Peter Kilmartin. According to a 2013 report from the Governors Highway Safety Association, forty-seven states and the District of Columbia are increasing public education efforts about the dangers of distracted driving, a 26 percent increase from 2010. States report that they are also using social media, including Twitter, YouTube, and Facebook, to educate motorists. "We have to get the message out to people not just young people but all people whether it is eating, drink[ing], [or] using electronic appliances it is all very dangerous while you are driving,"[52] says Robert Williams of the Maine State Police.

> "In order to change people's behaviors, we need to continually educate the public about the dangers of texting while driving."[51]
>
> —Peter Kilmartin, Rhode Island attorney general.

The Governors Highway Safety Association survey also found that many states are partnering with private businesses and government agencies to spread distracted driving messages. One of the programs being used in this fight is Ford Motor Company's Driving Skills for Life, which goes by the name Ford DSFL. The program has partnered with the Governors Highway Safety Association and more than forty states to actively engage teens in discussions of distracted driving and safe driving practices. The program features a website, hands-on driving events, and materials that focus on key safety issues, including driver distraction. "Over the last 10 years we have taken pride in our ability to adjust the curriculum to keep up with the constantly changing world awaiting teens and other new drivers,"[53] says Jim Graham, Ford DSFL manager.

Distracted driving is a problem for everyone on the road. Stiffer penalties will do little to change driver behavior, mainly because many people simply do not think they will be caught or do not understand the serious consequences of distracted driving. "It's more productive to treat distracted driving as a driver education problem,"[54] says Gary Biller, president of the National Motorists Association, a drivers' rights group. In order to make a real change in behavior, drivers need to be educated about the risks and consequences of their actions, as well as ways to make safer choices while driving.

Chapter Four

Do New Automotive Technologies Add to Distracted Driving Risks?

New Automotive Technologies Add to Distracted Driving Risks

- Complex entertainment and information systems built into cars divert a driver's attention away from the road.
- When technological devices are built into car dashboards, drivers have the false impression that using them while driving is safe.
- Studies have found that using voice-controlled technology is more distracting for drivers than holding a handheld cell phone.
- To reduce driver distraction, automakers should disable all nondriving functions and technology while a car is in motion.

The Debate at a Glance

New Automotive Technologies Do Not Add to Distracted Driving Risks

- New automotive technologies reduce distraction by allowing drivers to keep their hands on the wheel and eyes on the road.
- Built-in technologies replace handheld devices, eliminating distractions caused by drivers reaching for or operating these devices.
- Automakers have addressed safety concerns when designing in-car technologies, including voice control operation and other safety features that help drivers avoid accidents.

New Automotive Technologies Add to Distracted Driving Risks

"Technology has created more distractions."

—Peter Kilmartin, Rhode Island attorney general.

Quoted in Paul J. Spetrini, "RI's Texting While Driving Law Proving Ineffective," GoLocalProv, February 22, 2013. www.golocalprov.com.

Consider these questions as you read:

1. How persuasive is the argument that new automotive technologies increase distracted driving risks? Which arguments are strongest, and why?
2. Will this argument change how you use in-car technology? Why or why not?
3. How do you think automakers should balance safety and technology?

Editor's note: The discussion that follows presents common arguments made in support of this perspective, reinforced by facts, quotes, and examples taken from various sources.

Today's new cars have many in-car technologies that distract drivers from their primary focus while behind the wheel. Recognizing the safety risks caused by these technologies, the DOT urged automakers to limit their use when a car is in motion. This recommendation was included in the 2013 DOT guidelines to minimize in-vehicle distractions. "Distracted driving is a dangerous and deadly habit on America's roadways—that's why I've made it a priority to encourage people to stay focused behind the wheel," says US transportation secretary Ray LaHood. "These guidelines are a major step forward in identifying real solutions to tackle the issue of distracted driving for drivers of all ages."[55]

The DOT guidelines apply to communications, entertainment, information gathering, and navigation devices or functions that are not essential to operating the vehicle safely. The DOT wants automakers to disable functions that require visual and manual operation while the vehicle is in motion. The DOT's guidelines also recommend that no task take longer than two seconds. "We recognize that vehicle manufacturers want to build vehicles that include the tools and conveniences expected by today's American drivers," says NHTSA administrator David Strickland. "The guidelines we're proposing would offer real-world guidance to automakers to help them develop electronic devices that provide features consumers want—without disrupting a driver's attention or sacrificing safety."[56]

The DOT guidelines are voluntary and not enforceable under current laws. Although the government can issue warnings, automakers are free to ignore the warnings and continue to add new in-car technologies that further distract drivers.

Complex Entertainment and Navigation Systems

With the release of every new car model, automakers are adding more and more complex entertainment and navigation technologies. Some high-tech systems allow drivers to surf the Internet or update their social media status. According to market research firm IHS Automotive, approximately 23 million cars worldwide were connected to the Internet in 2013. By 2020 the number of Internet-connected vehicles is expected to reach 152 million. With Internet-connected cars, drivers can access popular websites and apps such as Google, Facebook, and Twitter. "Customers want to do other things while they are driving," says Steven Feit, a senior Honda engineer. "And they are used to consumer electronics, like phones and computer tablets, keeping up with what they want."[57]

> "Customers want to do other things while they are driving, . . . and they are used to consumer electronics, like phones and computer tablets, keeping up with what they want."[57]
>
> —Steven Feit, a senior Honda engineer.

Honda's Acura MDX model has built-in technology that delivers entertainment and Internet functions. Through voice commands, MDX drivers can select a destination for the car's navigation system or a phone number to call. The system also features a touch screen that allows a driver to select entertainment options while the vehicle is stationary, then press a single button to access them while driving. The system has a second screen for navigation, which can be controlled by voice commands or manually.

With this added technology, drivers are more distracted than ever. Frank Weith, general manager of Connected Services at Volkswagen, worries that driver distraction caused by in-car technology will lead to more accidents and injuries. "The last thing we want is customers changing their Facebook status or creating playlists while driving," says Weith. "The real value in driving is and always will be to get from one place to another."[58] LaHood also warns that in-car technology adds to driver distraction. "We don't have to choose between safety and technology," he says. "But while these devices may offer consumers new tools and features, automakers have a responsibility to ensure they don't divert a driver's attention away from the road."[59]

Automakers have a financial incentive to load new cars with complex entertainment and navigation systems. These systems appeal to young customers who want to be connected twenty-four hours a day, which helps the automakers sell more cars. While drivers like the services and connections these technologies provide, they are yet another dangerous distraction. Nicholas A. Ashford, a professor of technology and policy at the Massachusetts Institute of Technology, says, "This is irresponsible at best and pernicious at worst. Unfortunately and sadly, it is a continuation of the pursuit of profit over safety—for both drivers and pedestrians."[60]

Motivated by profits and consumer wish lists, automakers are feeding the frenzy for connected cars. Flashy car ads and commercials glamorize the idea of being connected 24/7. With such easy connections, drivers are having an even harder time saying no. "The problem in America is our cellphones are, in a sense, like alcohol. We're hooked on them and can't put them down when behind the wheel of the car, when we're driving," says LaHood. "We're hooked on these devices and can't put them down, anyplace, anytime, anywhere."[61]

Speech-to-Text Technology Increases Distraction

Many new in-car technologies rely on voice commands and speech-to-text systems that allow drivers to interact with electronics while keeping their hands on the steering wheel and eyes on the road. Research by the AAA Foundation for Traffic Safety has found that these voice-controlled systems create more distraction for drivers than listening to the radio or even than talking on a cell phone. In the graph, a workload rating of 1 is associated with a small increase in cognitive distraction; a workload rating of 2 is associated with a moderate but significant increase in cognitive distraction; and a workload rating of 3 is associated with a relatively high level of cognitive distraction.

Cognitive Distraction Scale

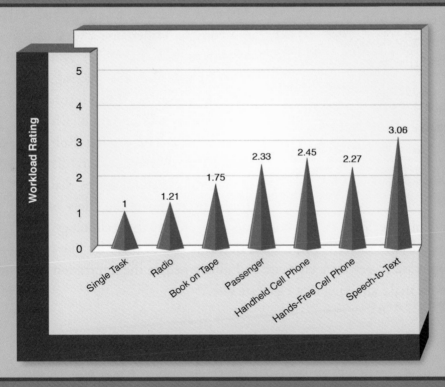

Source: AAA Foundation for Traffic Safety, "Measuring Cognitive Distraction in the Automobile," June 2013. www.aaafoundation.org.

False Impression of Safety

Most people assume that when a car arrives at a dealership's showroom, it has been tested and inspected for safety. All of the car's systems, from the brakes to the speedometer, are believed to be safe to use while driving. In-car technologies built into the car's dashboard are no different. Just because the technology is built in, many people have the false impression that these devices are safe to use while driving; otherwise, they would not have been included in the car.

In reality, many in-vehicle technologies are unsafe to use when a vehicle is in motion. In-vehicle entertainment and navigation systems often require drivers to look away from the road and at a console. Others use a joystick-like control to operate, which removes a driver's hand from the steering wheel. The operation of these technologies requires a driver's attention, which reduces the focus on driving. Rob Reynolds of FocusDriven, an anti–distracted driving organization, agrees that many drivers overestimate the safety of using in-vehicle technology. Reynolds says that putting the technology in cars gives drivers the false impression that it is safe to use. "It's like putting a filter on a very large cigarette and giving people the impression that it might make smoking that cigarette safe."[62]

> "There is a looming public safety crisis ahead with the future proliferation of these in-vehicle technologies. It's time to consider limiting new and potentially dangerous mental distractions built into cars, particularly with the common public misperception that hands-free means risk-free."[64]
>
> —Robert Darbelnet, AAA president.

Dangers of Voice-Controlled Systems

Some of the newest in-car technologies use voice-recognition or voice-control systems. These systems allow drivers to compose texts, select songs, or perform other tasks using voice commands. Although automakers have widely promoted voice-controlled systems and claim that they are safer than using a handheld phone, many safety experts disagree.

Recent research has found that voice-controlled systems can actually be more distracting than having a conversation on a handheld cell phone. In a 2013 study, researchers from the University of Utah compared activities such as listening to the radio, talking with passengers, using a cell phone, and using a voice-command system. They measured participants' brain waves, reaction times, and head and eye movements as they performed each task while driving. The researchers found that composing a text using a voice-command system was actually more distracting than all other activities. "A rush to voice-based interactions in the vehicle may have unintended consequences that adversely affect vehicle safety,"[63] the researchers concluded. The AAA Foundation for Traffic Safety, the study's sponsor, recommends that drivers not use in-vehicle speech-to-text systems. "There is a looming public safety crisis ahead with the future proliferation of these in-vehicle technologies. It's time to consider limiting new and potentially dangerous mental distractions built into cars, particularly with the common public misperception that hands-free means risk-free,"[64] says AAA president Robert Darbelnet.

Disable Nondriving Functions

Where driving is concerned, safety should always take priority over convenience. New in-vehicle technologies offer convenience but are dangerous distractions. In order to improve road safety, LaHood says that he would like to see all nondriving functions disabled when a car is moving. "If somebody is trying to dial a number, even if it's voice-activated, they're obviously distracted from what they're supposed to be doing, and in many instances, people are driving 50 or 60 miles per hour,"[65] he says. No amount of convenience or entertainment is worth the risk of accident, injury, or death.

New Automotive Technologies Do Not Add to Distracted Driving Risks

"Our goal is to expand the suite of connected services offered in our vehicles with careful consideration to make sure these new features and services are relevant, add value for customers and are seamlessly integrated so drivers can stay focused on the road."

—Mary Chan, president of General Motor's Global Connected Consumer unit.

Quoted in General Motors, "Five Questions with Mary Chan," July 3, 2013. http://media.gm.com.

Consider these questions as you read:

1. How persuasive is the argument that new automotive technologies do not add to distracted driving risks? Which arguments are strongest, and why?
2. What level of responsibility do you think automakers have for safety when designing in-car technology? Explain your answer.
3. Do you think in-car technology is a safer alternative to handheld cell phones, music players, or GPS devices? Why or why not?

Editor's note: The discussion that follows presents common arguments made in support of this perspective, reinforced by facts, quotes, and examples taken from various sources.

Today's drivers want to be connected as they travel. As drivers spend time in the car commuting each day, the ability to access smartphones and the Internet while on the move allows them to be more efficient. "You have access to it right there and to be able to do it hands-free—that way you can actually drive your vehicle and not worry about crashing—is important,"[66] says Dan Zinni, director of the Dayton Auto Show.

Responding to customer demand, automakers are developing new in-vehicle technologies that connect drivers to apps, entertainment, navigation, and the Internet. For example, the Ford Motor Company has developed the MyFord Touch and SYNC systems, which allow drivers to access information and entertainment functions using traditional buttons, a touch screen, or voice commands. At the same time, many in-vehicle technologies improve driver safety by eliminating the need for drivers to reach for and manipulate cell phones and other portable electronic devices. "We know people want to stay connected in their vehicles, so Ford is continuing to deliver that connectivity for them responsibly and safely," says Susan Cischke, Ford's group vice president of Sustainability, Environment and Safety Engineering. "Our SYNC research backs up what most of us instinctively know—that it is better while driving to place a call using a voice interface than dialing manually, because you can keep your hands on the wheel and eyes on the road."[67]

New Technologies Reduce Visual Distractions

Automakers are turning to new technologies to reduce visual distractions. Cars are being equipped with a wider use of voice commands that allow drivers to change radio stations, request directions to a specific location, or make a phone call. Voice commands give drivers the ability to operate infotainment systems without looking down at a console or handheld device. Delphi, a supplier of electronics for the automotive industry, says that it has developed systems that put important information in the driver's field of view and give drivers the ability to control major functions by either touching a button on the steering wheel or by using voice control. In some BMW models drivers can use voice commands to dictate e-mails or text messages. Other car models such as the Chevrolet Sonic compact car have a system that allows drivers to speak

> "We know people want to stay connected in their vehicles, so Ford is continuing to deliver that connectivity for them responsibly and safely."[67]
>
> —Susan Cischke, Ford's group vice president of Sustainability, Environment and Safety Engineering.

text messages that are translated into text on an iPhone connected to the car. More than half of all new cars will have some form of voice command technology by 2019, according to IMS Research, an electronics consulting firm.

Other new technologies use a heads-up display to show navigation routes, audio channels, and other information while still allowing drivers to keep their eyes focused on the road. The heads-up display projects light onto the windshield, which creates an image that appears just above the car's hood about 5 to 8 feet (1.5 to 2.4 m) beyond the windshield. For example, a heads-up display of a navigation tool can make a turn arrow appear overlaid on the road ahead, to show drivers where to turn. Heads-up displays are safer than handheld or even console-operated technologies because the driver's eyes do not need to shift between the display and the road. In addition, some heads-up displays can be operated with a gesture, such as a hand wave to silence a call, instead of reaching for a button.

Replacing Handheld Devices Improves Safety

Drivers want to stay connected wherever they go. Despite the risks, they are bringing their smartphones, MP3 players, and portable GPS devices into cars and using them while driving. Accidents occur when drivers reach for or operate these portable, handheld devices. "If you use a portable device, that level of distraction is considerably higher than when it is built into the car,"[68] says David Cole, chair emeritus of the Center for Automotive Research in Ann Arbor, Michigan. Instead of handheld devices, in-vehicle technologies allow drivers quick and safer ways to access information and stay connected in the car. "We are trying to give our customers what they want in a way that's going to be safe and make sense," says Steven Feit, a senior Honda engineer. "That's the balance we are trying to get to."[69]

Many in-car technologies can be operated with voice controls, which eliminates the need to reach for a device or look away from the road. Brad Hoffman, vice president of communications for Harman, an audio company, says that his company's research supports the use of voice con-

Users Approve of New Voice-Control Technology

According to a report from the AAA Foundation for Traffic Safety, one in five licensed drivers reports owning or regularly driving a vehicle that has a built-in voice-controlled system. The majority of users of these systems say they are not distracting, or only slightly distracting, to operate while driving.

Do you find it distracting to use this technology by speaking?

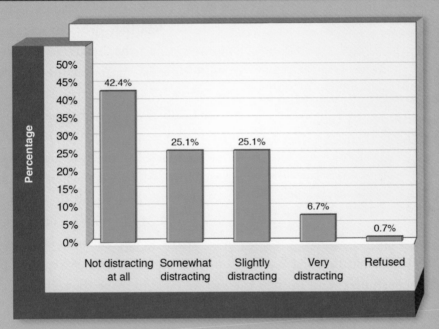

Base: Licensed drivers aged 16+ who reported that the vehicle they own or drive regularly has a voice-control system.

Source: AAA Foundation for Traffic Safety, "Distracted Driving and Perceptions of Hands-Free Technologies," November 2013. www.aaafoundation.org.

trols for in-car technology. "Our own research, as well as that from various institutions, shows that hands-free operation of in-vehicle devices is not sufficient for optimum safety," says Hoffman. "Well-designed devices must also offer eyes-free operation."[70] Voice control provides both.

Automakers Including Safety Features

Safety is a priority for automakers, who are trying to balance it with customer convenience, according to Ericka Pfeifer, a Ford Motor Company spokesperson. "They don't want you looking down at a map or reading text messages; they want it all to be audible so you can keep your eyes on the road and minimize that possibility for accidents,"[71] says Pfeifer.

In addition to designing safer, voice-controlled systems, automakers are also including new safety features in combination with in-car technologies. These features can help drivers avoid accidents. The Acura MDX, for instance, has sensors that warn drivers of potential collisions, alert them when they drift out of their lane, and apply the brakes to reduce speed if an accident appears likely. On some models, adaptive cruise control automatically stops the car if the vehicle in front of it stops suddenly. Other automakers block Internet use and entry into navigation functions when the car is moving. "We understand the stakes," says Gloria Bergquist, vice president for public affairs at the Alliance of Automobile Manufacturers, a Washington trade organization. "We can't stop what consumers want in their cars, so we have to make the technology less risky to use."[72]

> "We understand the stakes. . . . We can't stop what consumers want in their cars, so we have to make the technology less risky to use."[72]
>
> —Gloria Bergquist, vice president for public affairs at the Alliance of Automobile Manufacturers.

Connected Cars of the Future

In-car technology may be making roads even safer in the not-so-distant future. Built-in Internet capabilities and wireless connections may one day allow cars to connect with each other while on the road. Automakers and electronics companies envision the connected car to be able to communicate with other cars and the road itself in order to reduce and mitigate the risks of distracted drivers.

Some connected cars may even be able to use information from other cars and the road to drive themselves. Technology companies like Google and automakers are working to develop a self-driving car, also known as autonomous driving. In this model, computer systems would control the vehicle's operation. To help drivers avoid accidents, the car's computer would warn drivers when they drift out of a lane or get too close to another car. "Autonomous driving will certainly provide safety benefits," says Frank Weith. "There will be a slow transition—vehicle-to-vehicle communication needs to improve—but the infrastructure is quickly evolving."[73]

A Safer Way to Connect

Despite the serious risks of distracted driving, drivers continue to use cell phones, music players, and other electronics in the car. In-vehicle technologies offer a safer alternative, allowing drivers to reduce the amount of time they spend reaching for devices, manually dialing or texting, or looking down to read a text or dial a number. "Studies show voice-activated systems like SYNC offer significant safety benefits over hand-held manual devices," says John Shutko, a Ford technical specialist in Human Factors and Ergonomics. "If people are going to use nomadic devices [handheld wireless devices], Ford Motor Company wants to offer our customers a safer way to use them."[74]

Source Notes

Overview: High-Tech Distractions

1. Quoted in Aarti Shahani, "Does Google Glass Distract Drivers? The Debate Is On," *All Tech Considered* (blog), NPR, March 24, 2014. www.npr.org.

2. Quoted in Dan Levine, "Exclusive: Google Sets Roadblocks to Stop Distracted Driver Legislation," Reuters, February 25, 2014. www.reuters.com.

3. Quoted in Shahani, "Does Google Glass Distract Drivers? The Debate Is On."

4. Quoted in Shahani, "Does Google Glass Distract Drivers? The Debate Is On."

5. Quoted in Nicholas Bakalar, "Distracted Drivers and New Drivers a Perilous Mix," *Well* (blog), *New York Times*, January 2, 2014. http://well.blogs.nytimes.com.

6. Quoted in US Department of Transportation, "U.S. Transportation Secretary LaHood Issues 'Blueprint for Ending Distracted Driving,' Announces $2.4 Million for California, Delaware Pilot Projects," June 7, 2012. www.distraction.gov.

Chapter One: Do Hands-Free Devices Enhance Driver Safety?

7. Quoted in AMTA, "AMTA Dial Up Campaign to Promote Safe and Responsible Phone Use While Driving," April 9, 2014. www.amta.org.au.

8. Quoted in Carroll Lachnit, "Distraction Debate Drives Search for Solutions," Edmunds.com, September 17, 2010. www.edmunds.com.

9. Quoted in Ashley Halsey, "Maryland Hands-Free Law Takes Effect Friday," *Washington Post*, September 25, 2010. www.washingtonpost.com.

10. Quoted in Public News Service, "Will WI Be the Next State to Require Hands-Free Cell Phones for Drivers?," February 11, 2014. www.publicnewsservice.org.

11. Quoted in Lachnit, "Distraction Debate Drives Search for Solutions."

12. Quoted in National Safety Council, "National Safety Council Poll: 8 in 10 Drivers Mistakenly Believe Hands-Free Cell Phones Are Safer," April 1, 2014. www.nsc.org.

13. Quoted in University of Utah, "Hands-Free Talking and Texting Are Unsafe for Drivers, Study Shows," ScienceDaily, June 12, 2013. www.sciencedaily.com.

14. Quoted in University of Utah, "Hands-Free Talking and Texting Are Unsafe for Drivers, Study Shows."

15. Quoted in University of Utah, "Hands-Free Talking and Texting Are Unsafe for Drivers, Study Shows."

16. Quoted in Chris Kissell, "Pay Attention! 6 Causes of Distracted Driving," Fox Business, August 23, 2013. www.foxbusiness.com.

17. Quoted in Matt Richtel, "U.S. Safety Board Urges Cellphone Ban for Drivers," New York Times, December 13, 2011. www.nytimes.com.

18. Quoted in Angela Greiling Keane, "Brain Can't Text While Driving Even with Hands Free: AAA," Bloomberg, June 12, 2013. www.bloomberg.com.

Chapter Two: Should Cell Phone Use by Drivers Be Banned?

19. Quoted in Don Thompson, "California Cellphone Ban Reduced Traffic Related Deaths, Injuries, Berkeley Study Finds," Huffington Post, March 5, 2012. www.huffingtonpost.com.

20. Quoted in Paul J. Spetrini, "RI's Texting While Driving Law Proving Ineffective," GoLocalProv, February 22, 2013. www.golocalprov.com.

21. Quoted in University of Utah, "Drivers on Cell Phones Are as Bad as Drunks," June 29, 2006. http://unews.utah.edu.

22. Quoted in Sarah Rohrs, "Hands-Free Cell Phones Almost as Bad as Driving Drunk, Study Shows," *Huffington Post*, May 23, 2013. www.huffingtonpost.com.

23. Sheila G. Klauer et al., "Distracted Driving and Risk of Road Crashes Among Novice and Experienced Drivers," *New England Journal of Medicine*, January 2, 2014. www.nejm.org.

24. Quoted in Terence Corcoran, "N.Y. Family Who Lost Son Fights Distracted Driving," *USA Today*, May 29, 2013. www.usatoday.com.

25. Quoted in Mike M. Ahlers, "NTSB Recommends Full Ban on Use of Cell Phones While Driving," CNN, December 14, 2011. www.cnn.com.

26. Quoted in Katie Sullivan, "Texting Laws Ineffective, Hard to Enforce, Police Say," *Scranton (PA) Times-Tribune*, September 4, 2012. http://thetimes-tribune.com.

27. Quoted in Jim Gorzelany, "Forget Phones or Fast Food, More Drivers Cause Their Own Crashes," *Forbes*, April 3, 2013. www.forbes.com.

28. Quoted in Carol Cruzan Morton, "Why Cell Phone Bans Don't Work," *Science*, August 22, 2012. http://news.sciencemag.org.

29. Quoted in Gary Richards, "Texting, Handheld Phones: Distracted-Driving Crackdown Coming in April," *San Jose (CA) Mercury News*, March 16, 2013. www.mercurynews.com.

30. Quoted in HLDI News, "Texting Bans Don't Reduce Crashes; Effects Are Slight Crash Increases," Insurance Institute for Highway Safety, September 28, 2010. www.iihs.org.

31. Quoted in HLDI News, "Texting Bans Don't Reduce Crashes; Effects Are Slight Crash Increases."

32. Quoted in Matt Sedensky, "Cellphone Ban in Cars Could Be 'Impossible' to Enforce According to Law Enforcement," *Huffington Post*, December 16, 2011. www.huffingtonpost.com.

33. Quoted in Sedensky, "Cellphone Ban in Cars Could Be 'Impossible' to Enforce According to Law Enforcement."

34. Quoted in HLDI News, "Texting Bans Don't Reduce Crashes; Effects Are Slight Crash Increases."

Chapter Three: Would Stiffer Penalties Reduce Distracted Driving Threats?

35. Quoted in Shawn Ghuman, "States Consider Raising Fines for Distracted Driving," *USA Today*, June 26, 2012. http://usatoday30.usatoday.com.

36. Quoted in Robert Preidt, "Stricter Laws Might Reduce Aggressive Driving in Young Males: Study," *U.S. News & World Report*, June 14, 2014. http://health.usnews.com.

37. Quoted in Richards, "Texting, Handheld Phones: Distracted-Driving Crackdown Coming in April."

38. Quoted in National Safety Council, "Public Ready for Stiffer Penalties for Texting While Driving," June 23, 2014. www.nsc.org.

39. Quoted in Erin Cox, "O'Malley Signs 'Jake's Law,' Marijuana Decriminalization," *Maryland Politics* (blog), *Baltimore (MD) Sun*, April 14, 2014. www.baltimoresun.com.

40. Quoted in Cox, "O'Malley Signs 'Jake's Law,' Marijuana Decriminalization."

41. Quoted in ABC News, "Felony Charges in Distracted Driving Case," April 16, 2014. http://abcnews.go.com.

42. Quoted in ABC News, "Felony Charges in Distracted Driving Case."

43. Quoted in Denis Cuff and Joe Rodriguez, "Gov. Brown Vetoes Bill Increasing Distracted Drivers' Fine," *Vallejo (CA) Times-Herald*, September 8, 2011. www.timesheraldonline.com.

44. Quoted in Elsevier, "Distracted Driving Among Teens Threatens Public Health and Safety," ScienceDaily, April 17, 2014. www.sciencedaily.com.

45. Quoted in Cuff and Rodriguez, "Gov. Brown Vetoes Bill Increasing Distracted Drivers' Fine."

46. Quoted in Hands Free Info, "Calif. Governor Again Rejects Fine Hikes," October 2, 2012. http://handsfreeinfo.com.

47. Quoted in Cuff and Rodriguez, "Gov. Brown Vetoes Bill Increasing Distracted Drivers' Fine."

48. Quoted in *Fleet Alert*, "Worst States for Distracted Drivers," May 2010. www.alertdriving.com.

49. Quoted in Spetrini, "RI's Texting While Driving Law Proving Ineffective."

50. Jay Winsten, "Stopping Distracted Driving: What Will It Take?," *Huffington Post*, November 1, 2013. www.huffingtonpost.com.

51. Quoted in Spetrini, "RI's Texting While Driving Law Proving Ineffective."

52. Quoted in Vivien Leigh, "State Police Crack Down on Distracted Driving," WCSH6.com, April 10, 2014. www.wcsh6.com.

53. Quoted in Governors Highway Safety Association, "Ford Driving Skills for Life Advanced Driving Skills Program Begins Second Decade with New Content, Technology," March 20, 2014. www.ghsa.org.

54. Quoted in Ghuman, "States Consider Raising Fines for Distracted Driving."

Chapter Four: Do New Automotive Technologies Add to Distracted Driving Risks?

55. Quoted in US Department of Transportation, "US Department of Transportation Proposes 'Distraction' Guidelines for Automakers," February 16, 2012. www.dot.gov.

56. Quoted in US Department of Transportation, "US Department of Transportation Proposes 'Distraction' Guidelines for Automakers."

57. Quoted in Bill Vlasic, "Designing Dashboards with Fewer Distractions," *New York Times*, July 5, 2013. www.nytimes.com.

58. Quoted in Meg Fry, "Wi-Fi over Four-Wheel Drive? Carmakers Are Shifting Focus," NJBiz, April 14, 2014. www.njbiz.com.

59. Quoted in Claire Martin, "New In-Car Tech Rolled Out Despite Distracted-Driver Guidelines," *Exhaust Notes* (blog), MSN, May 23, 2012. http://editorial.autos.msn.com.

60. Quoted in Caroline Knorr, "Driving Distractions: The Dangers of In-Car Electronics," *Common Sense Blog*, Common Sense Media, January 7, 2010. www.commonsensemedia.org.

61. Quoted in Matt Richtel, "LaHood Says Companies Must Wake Up to Distracted Driving," *Bits* (blog), *NYTimes.com*, July 24, 2013. http://bits.blogs.nytimes.com.

62. Quoted in Martin, "New In-Car Tech Rolled Out Despite Distracted-Driver Guidelines."

63. Quoted in Hands Free Info, "In-Dash Hands-Free Flunks Test," June 12, 2013. http://handsfreeinfo.com.

64. Quoted in Hands Free Info, "In-Dash Hands-Free Flunks Test."

65. Quoted in Richtel, "LaHood Says Companies Must Wake Up to Distracted Driving."

66. Quoted in Dave Larson, "Tech-Loaded Cars Part of Distracted Driver Debate," *Springfield (OH) News-Sun*, February 22, 2012. www.springfieldnewssun.com.

67. Quoted in Ford Motor Company, "Study: Ford SYNC™ Reduces Driving Distractions, Helps Drivers Keep Eyes on Road," February 4, 2009. http://ophelia.sdsu.edu.

68. Quoted in Larson, "Tech-Loaded Cars Part of Distracted Driver Debate."

69. Quoted in Bill Vlasic, "Designing Dashboards with Fewer Distractions," *New York Times*, July 5, 2013. www.nytimes.com.

70. Quoted in Lachnit, "Distraction Debate Drives Search for Solutions."

71. Quoted in Larson, "Tech-Loaded Cars Part of Distracted Driver Debate."

72. Quoted in Vlasic, "Designing Dashboards with Fewer Distractions."

73. Quoted in Fry, "Wi-Fi over Four-Wheel Drive? Carmakers Are Shifting Focus."

74. Quoted in Chris Shunk, "Ford Says New Study Shows SYNC Leads to Fewer Distracted Drivers," *Autoblog*, February 6, 2009. www.autoblog.com.

Distracted Driving Facts

Cell Phones and Driving

- According to the Centers for Disease Control and Prevention, 25 percent of drivers in the United States report that they talk on their cell phone regularly or fairly often while driving.
- At any given daylight moment across America, approximately 660,000 drivers are using cell phones or manipulating electronic devices while driving, reports the NHTSA.
- Researchers at Carnegie Mellon University report that driving while using a cell phone reduces the amount of brain activity associated with driving by 37 percent.
- Nearly 7 out of 10 drivers report talking on the phone while driving, says the Governors Highway Safety Association.

Risks of Distracted Driving

- According to NHTSA statistics, 3,328 people were killed in distracted driving accidents in 2012.
- According to the NHTSA, an estimated 421,000 people were injured in motor vehicle accidents caused by distracted driving in 2012.
- According to researchers at VTTI, text messaging creates a crash risk twenty-three times worse than driving while not distracted.
- According to VTTI, reaching for a phone, dialing, and texting increase the risk of getting into a crash by three times.
- The Governors Highway Safety Association reports that nine out of ten licensed drivers believe that drivers talking on cell phones are a threat to their personal safety.

Novice Drivers and Distraction

- Driver inexperience and driver distraction have been identified as significant factors that affect the safety of young drivers.

- Drivers in their twenties make up 27 percent of the distracted drivers in fatal crashes, according to the NHTSA.
- The University of Michigan Transportation Research Institute reports that one-quarter of teens respond to a text message once or more every time they drive and that 20 percent of teens and 10 percent of parents admit that they have extended, multimessage text conversations while driving.
- Ten percent of all drivers under age twenty involved in fatal crashes were reported as distracted at the time of the crash. This age group has the largest proportion of drivers who were distracted, says the NHTSA.
- Thirty-eight states and the District of Columbia ban all cell phone use by novice drivers.
- Teens who engage in distracting behaviors while driving are more likely to have parents who also engage in distracting behaviors in the car.
- Only about one out of five young drivers thinks that texting makes no difference to their driving performance, according to the NHTSA.
- An NHTSA survey found that 68 percent of young drivers aged eighteen to twenty are willing to answer incoming phone calls on some, most, or all driving trips.

Prevention Efforts

- In 2012 forty states reported that distracted driving was a serious enough concern to be addressed in their state's Strategic Highway Safety Plan, a 43 percent increase over three years earlier, according to the Governors Highway Safety Association.
- In 2012 forty-seven states and the District of Columbia reported having taken steps to educate the public about the threat of distracted driving, according to the Governors Highway Safety Association.
- According to the Governors Highway Safety Association, twenty-nine states report that lack of funding for enforcement is a major obstacle to prioritizing distracted driving prevention.

Related Organizations and Websites

Centers for Disease Control and Prevention (CDC)
1600 Clifton Rd.
Atlanta, GA 30333
phone: (800) 232-4636
website: www.cdc.gov

The CDC works with partners around the country and the world to monitor health, detect and investigate health problems, conduct research into health issues, and promote healthy behaviors, including those related to cell phone use and safe driving.

CTIA
1400 Sixteenth St. NW, Suite 600
Washington, DC 20036
phone: (202) 736-3200 • fax: (202) 785-0721
website: www.ctia.org

Founded in 1984, this international nonprofit membership organization supports the wireless communications industry and provides information on cell phone–related issues and laws, including cell phones and driving.

Distraction.gov
National Highway Traffic Safety Administration
1200 New Jersey Ave. SE
Washington, DC 20590
website: www.distraction.gov

Distraction.gov is the official US government website from the National Highway Traffic Safety Administration focused on the issue of distracted driving. The site offers up-to-date information, facts, and statistics regarding distracted driving, including the use of cell phones.

Don't Drive and Text
222 N. Main St., Suite A
Bryan, TX 77803
website: http://dontdriveandtext.org

This organization provides information on the dangers of texting and driving in order to educate people about the practice.

Governors Highway Safety Association (GHSA)
444 N. Capitol St. NW, Suite 722
Washington, DC 20001-1534
phone: (202) 789-0942 • fax: (202) 789-0946
website: www.ghsa.org

The GHSA provides leadership and advocacy for the states and territories to improve traffic safety, influence national policy, enhance program management, and promote best practices.

Insurance Institute for Highway Safety (IIHS)
1005 N. Glebe Rd., Suite 800
Arlington, VA 22201
phone: (703) 247-1500 • fax: (703) 247-1588
website: www.iihs.org

The IIHS is an independent nonprofit scientific and educational organization dedicated to reducing the losses—deaths, injuries, and property damage—from crashes on the nation's roads.

National Safety Council
1121 Spring Lake Dr.
Itasca, IL 60143-3201
phone: (800) 621-7615 • fax: (630) 285-1315
website: www.nsc.org

This organization aims to save lives by preventing injuries and deaths at work, in homes, and in communities and provides information on a variety of safety issues, including distracted driving.

Virginia Tech Transportation Institute
3500 Transportation Research Plaza
Blacksburg, VA 24061
phone: (540) 231-1500 • fax: (540) 231-1555
website: www.vtti.vt.edu

The institute conducts research aimed at saving lives, time, and money in the transportation field, including research on the use of cell phones while driving.

World Health Organization (WHO)
Avenue Appia 20
1211 Geneva 27, Switzerland
phone: 41 22 791 21 11 • fax: 41 22 791 31 11
website: www.who.int

WHO supports research and provides information on a wide variety of health issues, including those related to cell phone use and distracted driving.

For Further Research

Books

Michele Siuda Jacques, ed., *Teen Driving*. Farmington Hills, MI: Green-haven, 2012.

Stefan Kiesbye, ed., *Cell Phones and Driving*. Farmington Hills, MI: Greenhaven, 2010.

Stefan Kiesbye, ed., *Distracted Driving*. Farmington Hills, MI: Green-haven, 2012.

Patricia Netzley, *How Serious Is Teen Drunk and Distracted Driving?* San Diego, CA: ReferencePoint, 2013.

Gail Stewart, *Cell Phones and Distracted Driving*. San Diego, CA: Refer-encePoint, 2014.

Internet Sources

G.A. Fitch et al., *The Impact of Hand-Held and Hands-Free Cell Phone Use on Driving Performance and Safety-Critical Event Risk*. Washington, DC: National Highway Traffic Safety Administration, 2013. www.dis traction.gov/download/811757.pdf.

Arthur H. Goodwin et al., *Distracted Driving Among Newly Licensed Teen Drivers*. Washington, DC: AAA Foundation for Traffic Safety, 2012. www.distraction.gov/download/DistractedDrivingAmongNewly LicensedTeenDrivers.pdf.

Sheila G. Klauer et al., "Distracted Driving and Risk of Road Crash-es Among Novice and Experienced Drivers," *New England Journal of Medicine*, January 2, 2014. www.nejm.org/doi/full/10.1056/NEJM sa1204142.

Amanda Lenhart et al., "Teens and Mobile Phones," Pew Internet & American Life Project, April 20, 2010. www.pewinternet.org/2010/04 /20/teens-and-mobile-phones.

National Highway Traffic Safety Administration, *Blueprint for Ending Distracted Driving*. Washington, DC: National Highway Traffic Safety Administration, 2012. www.distraction.gov/download/811629.pdf.

National Highway Traffic Safety Administration, "Distracted Driving 2011," April 2013. www-nrd.nhtsa.dot.gov/Pubs/811737.pdf.

Aaron Smith, "Americans and Text Messaging," Pew Research Internet Project, September 19, 2011. www.pewinternet.org/2011/09/19/amer icans-and-text-messaging.

World Health Organization, *Mobile Phone Use: A Growing Problem of Driver Distraction*. Geneva: World Health Organization, 2011. www .who.int/violence_injury_prevention/publications/road_traffic/distract ed_driving_en.pdf.

Index